PLEASE, THANK YOU, YES, OKAY
AND OTHER NICE THINGS TO SAY

PLEASE, THANK YOU, YES, OKAY
AND OTHER NICE THINGS TO SAY

WRITTEN AND ILLUSTRATED BY

LESLIE PRESCOTT

To Melissa,
Best Wishes!
Leslie Prescott

Riverhaven Books
www.RiverhavenBooks.com

Published in the United States by Riverhaven Books
www.RiverhavenBooks.com

ISBN: 978-1-937588-26-7

Printed in the United States of America
by Country Press, Lakeville, Massachusetts

for my mother and father
who taught me well

EVEN THOUGH I AM YOUNG,
I CAN MAKE SMILES EACH DAY
BEING KIND AND HELPFUL
AND MINDING WHAT I SAY.

MOMMY TELLS ME, "IT'S TIME TO PUT YOUR TOYS AWAY."

I BEGIN WITH MY RED CAR
AND I SAY, "OKAY."

GRANDMA SENDS A PRESENT,
OR SOMETIMES SHE SENDS TWO.

I ALWAYS CALL HER ON THE PHONE TO SAY, "THANK YOU."

DADDY IS TALKING WITH HIS
FRIEND BY THE BIG TREE;

IF I NEED TO TALK TO HIM,
I SAY, "EXCUSE ME."

MY LITTLE SISTER, BETTY,
CANNOT TIE HER SHOE.

I KNEEL DOWN NEXT TO HER
AND SAY, "I WILL HELP YOU."

AT LUNCH GRANDPA ASKS,
"WOULD YOU LIKE
SOME MAC AND CHEESE?"

I TUCK IN MY NAPKIN
AND THEN I SAY, "YES, PLEASE!"

WHEN MY FRIEND, JORDAN,
TELLS ME, "I LIKE YOU,"

I SMILE AT HIM AND SAY,
"I REALLY LIKE YOU, TOO!"

PLEASE, THANK YOU, YES, OKAY...PLEASE, THANK YOU, YES, OKAY...

I TRY TO REMEMBER
PLEASE, THANK YOU, YES, OKAY,

PLEASE, THANK YOU, YES, OKAY...PLEASE, THANK YOU, YES, OKAY...

PLEASE, THANK YOU, YES, OKAY...PLEASE, THANK YOU, YES, OKAY...

AND OTHER NICE THINGS TO SAY
EACH AND EVERY DAY!

PLEASE, THANK YOU, YES, OKAY...PLEASE, THANK YOU, YES, OKAY...

CAN <u>YOU</u> THINK
OF SOME NICE
THINGS TO SAY?

SOME NICE
THINGS I SAY:

ALWAYS REMEMBER TO MAKE SOMEONE'S DAY

BY BEING KIND AND MINDING WHAT YOU SAY